IN SPACE

Moon

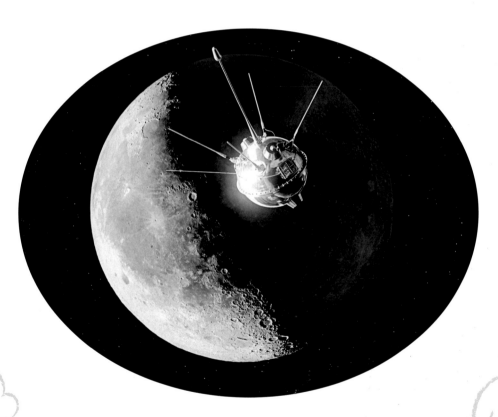

Chris Oxlade

Explore the world with **Popcorn** - your complete first non-fiction library.

Look out for more titles in the **Popcorn** range. All books have the same format of simple text and striking images. Text is carefully matched to the pictures to help readers to identify and understand key vocabulary.
www.waylandbooks.co.uk/popcorn

Published in 2013 by Wayland

Wayland
338 Euston Road
London NW1 3BH

Wayland Australia
Level 17/207 Kent Street
Sydney NSW 2000

Editor: Julia Adams
Designer: Robert Walster
Picture researcher: Julia Adams

British Library Cataloguing in Publication Data
Oxlade, Chris.
   Moon. -- (Popcorn. In space)
   1. Moon--Juvenile literature.
   I. Title II. Series
   523.3-dc22

ISBN 978 0 7502 6837 0

This edition first published in 2012 by Wayland.
Reprinted in 2013

Wayland is a division of Hachette Children's Books, an
Hachette UK Company
www.hachette.co.uk

Printed and bound in China

Acknowledgements:
iStockphoto: 4, 5, 23 tr, 23 bl; NASA 19;
NASA/JPL/USGS front cover, 6;
NASA/Harrison H. Schmitt 2, 21; NASA/JPL
7; NASA/Wes Higgins 9; NASA/Apollo 16
Crew 11; NASA/Apollo 11 Crew 20;
Science Photo Library: Larry Landolfi 8,
NASA 17, Detlev Van Ravenswaay 1, 18;
Shutterstock: Ken HIrst 12, Hashim
Pudiyapura 14, Brad Thompson 16, Daniel
Zuckerkandel 23 tl, Dmitry Kosterev 23br;
Illustrations: Graham Rich

Contents

The night sky

When you look at the night sky, you can see many stars shining. On a clear night, you can see the Moon, too.

Night-time begins when the Sun has set.

The Moon is much bigger than the stars.
It looks bright in the night sky.

When you look at the Moon through
a telescope you can see its surface.

What is the Moon?

The Moon is the Earth's nearest neighbour in space. It is a huge ball of rock.

The shape of the Moon is called a sphere.

We live on Earth. When you look at Earth from space, it is a big ball, too. But it is made up of water and land.

The Earth is four times bigger than the Moon.

Earth

Moon

On the Moon

There is no water and no air on the Moon. This is why no life can survive there.

The surface of the Moon is very rocky and dusty.

The Moon's surface has lots of craters and mountains. The craters look like big holes.

This is Crater Tycho. It is so huge that you can even see it from Earth!

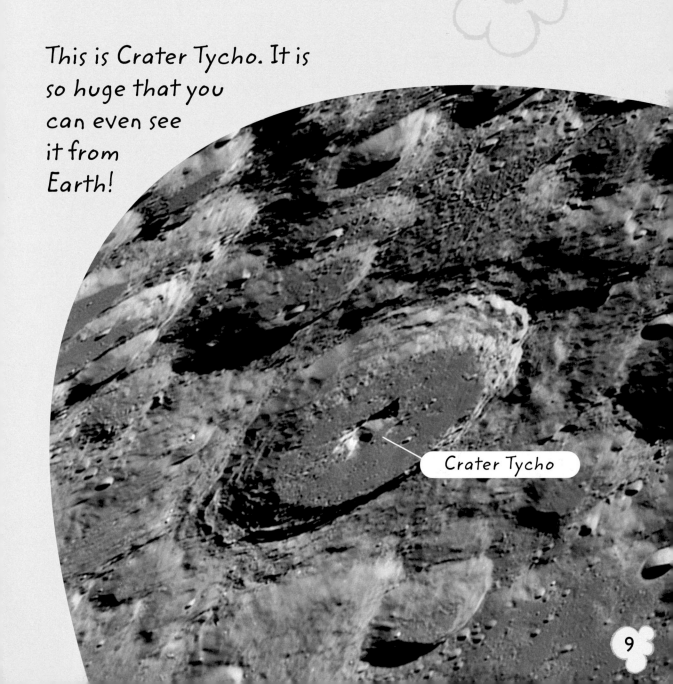

Crater Tycho

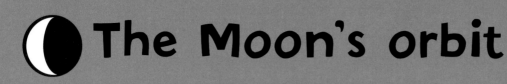 The Moon's orbit

The Moon moves around the Earth in a giant circle. The circle is called an orbit.

Earth

Moon

Moon's orbit

The Moon takes 27 days to orbit the Earth once. The same side of the Moon always faces the Earth. We never see the other side. It is called the far side.

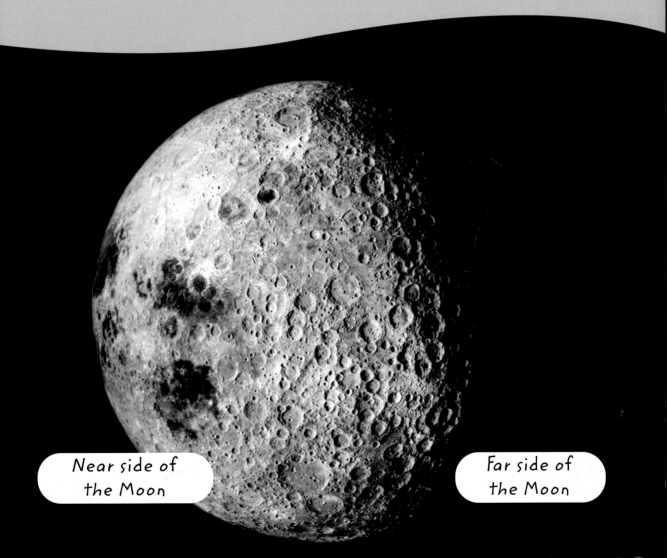

Near side of the Moon

Far side of the Moon

How the Moon shines

At night the Moon looks very bright,
but it does not make its own light.
It is lit up by the Sun.

The Sun shines on
one side of the
Moon only.

We see the Moon because it reflects the light from the Sun. The light that the Moon reflects is called moonlight.

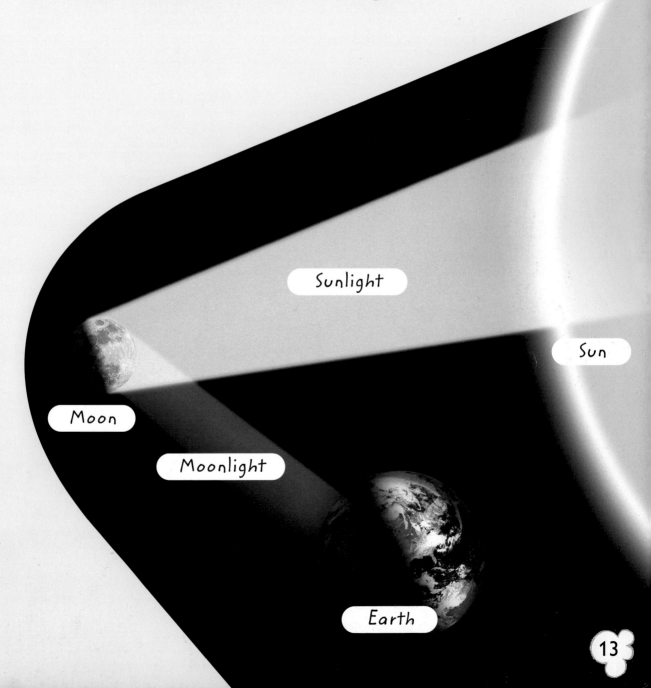

Sunlight

Sun

Moon

Moonlight

Earth

Changing shape

The Sun only lights up one side of the Moon. The other side is in darkness. From the Earth, we only see the half that is lit.

As the Moon orbits the Earth it seems to change shape. This is because we see different amounts of the side that is lit up.

The blue line shows you which part of the Moon you can see from Earth.

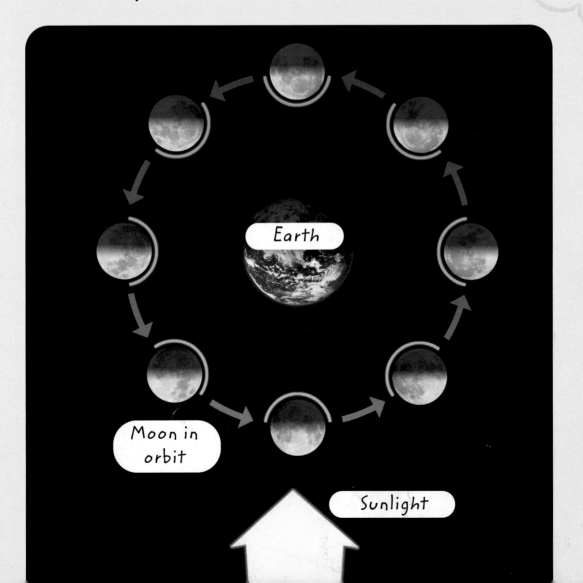

Earth

Moon in orbit

Sunlight

Full Moon and new Moon

Sometimes we see the whole side of the Moon that is lit up by the Sun. This is called a full Moon.

We see a full Moon once every 27 days.

Sometimes we see only a tiny part of the lit side of the Moon. This is called a new Moon.

This shape is called a crescent.

Visiting the Moon

Many robot spacecraft have visited the Moon. These spacecraft are called probes. They take photographs and send information about the Moon back to Earth.

The Luna 1 spacecraft visited the Moon in 1959.

Astronauts have also visited the Moon.
They flew to the Moon in a spacecraft.
Some flew around the Moon and some
landed on the Moon.

An Apollo
spacecraft on
the way to
the Moon.

The first
time astronauts
landed on the
Moon was
in 1969.

Landing on the Moon

Astronauts landed on the Moon to explore its surface. They wore spacesuits because there is no air to breathe on the Moon.

Buzz Aldrin was one of the first men to land on the Moon.

The astronauts spent 21 hours on the Moon. They collected rocks from the surface and many tests.

This astronaut is riding a lunar buggy.

Some people think it will be possible to live on the Moon one day.

Match the Moon shapes!

Look at the Moon shapes on this page. Can you match them to the pictures of the Moon on the right?

New Moon

Crescent

Half Moon

Full Moon

A

B

C

D

Glossary

astronaut a person who travels into space

crater a dish-shaped hole in the surface of the Moon

far side the side of the Moon that we cannot see from Earth

near side the side of the Moon that we can see from Earth

orbit the path of the Moon around the Earth, or to go round the Earth

Index